I0080587

#I

SURVIVED

30 Day Devotional for Millennials

QIANA BELL

Copyright ©2019 Qiana S. Bell

All rights reserved. No part of this book may be reproduced or used in any manner without written permission of the copyright owner except for the use of brief quotations in a book review.

First paperback edition, August 2019
Published by Qiana Bell

Book Design by: Kanika Harris
passionservicesinc@gmail.com
Book Editor: Val Pugh-Love
www.valpughlove.com

Printed in the United States of America

Introduction

When I was a junior at Grambling State University, I fell for a young man who was in my Advanced English course. One day after class, I was in my dorm room watching Tiger Channel - a GSU channel. There was a talk show on, and the topic was different faiths or religions on campus. Who should be on the panel but the young man I'd fallen for. While listening to the discussion, not only did I find out that he was married, but I also learned that he was Muslim. I'll never forget the statement he made on the show that day. He said that when he would ask his friends why they were Christians, not one of them could give a clear concise answer. Wow! That was alarming!

Sixteen years later, God dropped this devotional into my spirit. Millennials are leaving the church and are turning their backs on God at an astounding rate. I even thought about leaving the church and God. Honestly, it wasn't that long ago that I pondered that decision. You see, my qualifications for writing this devotional are not because I am perfect, but because I am imperfect. Right now, as I'm writing this book, I'm in the valley of my life. However, what I am assured of is that God had a plan for healing me as I write this and a plan for healing you as you read. We are on this journey together.

In this devotional, I will be as transparent as God allows. Most of the issues I'll discuss are either my own issues or the issues of someone who is close to me. I encourage you to use the Message Bible for clarity and understanding as you read along. I will give you two model prayers that will go along with each devotional. I'm not here to preach nor am I here to condemn. I am only here to help restore your faith in God and in the church.

Model Prayers

The first prayer is to be prayed before you open your bible and devotional. The second prayer is to be prayed after you've read your scriptures and devotional for the day. You must make time to really get the full benefit from this experience. The second prayer is quite different from the first prayer. Again, these are just model prayers. You may add or take away where you see fit.

Before Devotional and Bible Study Prayer

Father God in Heaven, I thank you for this day and for this time. I repent for everything I've said, thought, and done that did not bring Glory to your name. I ask for your forgiveness. As I read the word of God today, allow the word of God to read me so that change and transformation can come forth in my life. Blood tip my ears and break up the stony ground of my heart so that I may not only hear from you, but that I would also receive your word. In Jesus' name. Amen

After Devotional and Bible Study Prayer

1. 5-minute Praise - Thank God for what's He's done. You can even sing a song of praise.
2. 5-minute Repentance - Repent of all sins and trespasses, include that day's devotional subject.
3. 5-min Forgiveness - After you repent, you must ask for forgiveness.
4. 20-minute Intercession - Pray for your family members, church family, friends, and others.

5. 20-minute Prayer for Yourself - Lay your needs before God. Include all needs because He already knows what they are.
6. 5-minute Praise - Praise Him in advance for what He's going to do!

I'm not saying that you have to pray for a full hour, but be sure to stick to the structure of the prayer. Eventually, you may find yourself praying for over an hour - I know I have. These prayers will change how you view your prayer life. Before you dive into the devotional, I need you to do two things. First, commit to reading this devotional for the next 30 days. Secondly, open your heart to receive what God is saying. Will this process be easy? Probably not. Will it cause me to address and confess some issues? Yes, it will. However, even with being uncomfortable, just know that what's not addressed can't be resolved. Moreover, where there is no resolution, healing can't take place.

Now, take a deep breath, exhale, and get ready to be set free, restored, and healed.

Day 1
Ezekiel 37:1-14

A few months ago, my mother preached a sermon about Elijah in the desert with dry bones. In my mind, I always envisioned that there was only one skeleton perfectly in place and that Elijah only needed to speak to it. However, while my mother was preaching, she gave a different picture and therefore a different perspective. In her demonstration, the desert was full of scattered bones from different corpses. They had been scattered due to the elements and the animals picking over them. She said that when God gave Elijah the prophesy to give to the bones, no matter their location, the bones had to return to their original frame and back to their original position in the body.

Perhaps you feel like you're in the desert right now and that you're all alone. All your hopes, dreams, and visions are scattered around you, dry and lifeless. Your relationship with God may even be suffering because of your desert. The desert experience may even run over into the life of your family, friends, and employment. Allow God to offer you hope today. When God posed the question to Elijah, "Can these bones live?" Elijah had the only right answer: "God only thou knowest." God sees and knows everything that you are going through and experiencing. He is not ignorant of anything. Because He knows and see all things, He is the only one that can fix it. Think about it. How many other sources have you tried to use to fix your issue? How many books outside of the bible have you read to solve your problem? How many have worked?

Just as God gave Elijah the power to speak into the desert, He can give you the same authority to speak into your own life. Remember that God has no respecter of persons. What He did for Elijah and the children of Israel, surely, He can do for you. Ask God for forgiveness and direction, hold your head up, and watch Him work on your behalf. He will not only pull your life back together, but He'll breathe fresh life into you... all while you're in the valley.

Use the space below to write about how this devotional made you feel. Have you survived a situation like this? What changes do you think you should make in your life?

_____

_____

_____

_____

_____

_____

_____

_____

_____

_____

_____

_____

_____

_____

_____

_____

_____

_____

_____

_____

_____

_____

Day 2
Proverbs 4:25-27

I recently read a meme that said, "Don't let your food get cold watching someone else's plate." In other words, keep your eyes on your own prize. Too often, especially today, we compare ourselves to what and where the world says we should be. By a certain age, we should be married, have kids, and have reached our career goals. But, who set this standard, and why are we abiding by it? I was very guilty of this same thing for a long time. I would look at friends who perhaps were younger than I was, yet they had met all of life's standards. Whenever I would fall prey to this thought process, the enemy would immediately cause me to fall into a depression. I would have the greatest pity parties playing the greatest pity party hits. God would always have to come and say, "Stop looking to the left or right. Keep your eyes straight ahead."

In other words, He was simply telling me that if I kept my focus on Him then I wouldn't have time to focus on what everyone else around me was doing. In God's loving manner, He reminded me that I have my own race to run, and I have no time for distractions. If you've been on the "hamster's wheel" trying to keep up with the world's standards of where you should be in life, let me encourage you to STOP! Get off, breath deep, and refocus on God. Allow Him to direct your path. After all, He knows your beginning and your ending.

Use the space below to write about how this devotional made you feel. Have you survived a situation like this? What changes do you think you should make in your life?

_____
_____
_____
_____
_____
_____
_____
_____
_____
_____
_____
_____
_____
_____
_____
_____
_____
_____
_____
_____
_____
_____
_____
_____
_____
_____
_____
_____
_____
_____

Day 3

Psalms 139:13-16
Isaiah 26:3

Raise your hand if you've ever asked yourself, "What's wrong with me?" I have. I've literally picked myself apart mentally or stood in the mirror and physically picked myself apart. Why am I overweight? Why don't I look like my sisters? Why are my arms so big? Why is there a hump in my back? These are all questions I've asked myself. However, God created us and loves us just as we are. Despite how we feel about ourselves, we are marvelous because we were made in His image. So, let go of that poor self-image and remember that you were created from hands that shaped this beautiful world. Just as He said whenever He created something, "It is good," He said the same thing when He created you - a designer's original.

I've also realized that everyone does not struggle with self-esteem or self-awareness the same way. Perhaps you're okay with yourself physically, but you're a mess mentally. Maybe you battle with past mistakes and decisions that were disastrous. The bible tells us that the enemy is the accuser of the brethren. When an old mistake comes up and you start replaying it, it is the enemy that is toying with your mind. Rebuke the devil and remind him and yourself that you are not your mistakes. Furthermore, ask God to give you the wisdom and knowledge to see yourself as He sees you.

Use the space below to write about how this devotional made you feel. Have you survived a situation like this? What changes do you think you should make in your life?

_____
_____
_____
_____
_____
_____
_____
_____
_____
_____
_____
_____
_____
_____
_____
_____
_____
_____
_____
_____
_____
_____
_____
_____
_____
_____
_____
_____
_____
_____
_____
_____
_____
_____

Day 4
Proverbs 3:5-6

I try to be as transparent as possible. Thus far, I hope you find that to be true. This devotional will be no different from the others. While I'm writing, I have several decisions to make. Should I relinquish my lease and move? Is it time to purchase a new car? The most important one, however, is: Should I file for divorce? It seems in every area of my life there is a question lurking, and some questions seem to need immediate answers. Nevertheless, no matter how urgent the situation or question looks, one thing I have learned is to **NEVER** make a decision without consulting God **FIRST**. *Never* and *first* are both capitalized and bold because I want to stress the importance of consulting God before making decisions.

We tend to make plans for our lives without God's input (consultation). However, we will take Him the plan that we've come up with and ask Him to bless it. If we will simply go before Him with the question or problem and let Him lead and guide us, then we will find ourselves in His will instead of outside of it. When we are in His will, there is no need for the cleanup process that often happens when we direct our own path. If were really honest with ourselves, we would admit how limited we think. Rarely do we think a decision all the way through. Too often our thought process stops at the point in the plan were our desires are satisfied. We rarely contemplate the consequences of our actions. It's timeout for limited thinking and failing to consult God.

Make a conscious decision to never lean to your own understanding again. Whenever you must decide on something, remind yourself that your thinking and understanding is limited, and that God is all-knowing and all-seeing. He always has your best interest at heart, so allow Him to help you think before you act.

Use the space below to write about how this devotional made you feel. Have you survived a situation like this? What changes do you think you should make in your life?

_____

_____

_____

_____

_____

_____

_____

_____

_____

_____

_____

_____

_____

_____

_____

_____

_____

_____

_____

_____

_____

_____

_____

Day 5
Matthew 18:21-22

Sigh... It took me two days to write this devotional. I'm sure you're wondering why. Well, if you recall from the previous devotional, I'm pondering divorce. In my marriage, things have transpired that would lead one to believe that it can't be resuscitated. Some have byproducts of bitterness and anger. Along with bitterness and anger, unforgiveness joins the equation. Unforgiveness is a dangerous emotion. Doctors often tell their patients that emotional sickness can lead to physical ailments. It can control your every thought and cause hinderance in your life. As a result, self-growth cannot occur, and too often one might find themselves stagnate.

Don't get me wrong. I understand that human beings can inflict horrendous acts on one another that can cause forgiveness to be the furthest thing from our minds. That statement may have even prompted you to relive something that you or someone else may have said and done in a fit of anger. However, allow me to offer this bit of advice. Pray daily and ask God to help you forgive yourself and the person that hurt or angered you. This can't be done in our own strength. We need a higher power to help us accomplish what seems to be the unobtainable. Therefore, we must seek God to assist us with forgiveness just as we need Him in decision-making. Forgiveness is for you, for your health, and for your peace.

Use the space below to write about how this devotional made you feel. Have you survived a situation like this? What changes do you think you should make in your life?

_____
_____
_____
_____
_____
_____
_____
_____
_____
_____
_____
_____
_____
_____
_____
_____
_____
_____
_____
_____
_____
_____
_____
_____
_____
_____
_____
_____
_____
_____
_____
_____

Day 6

Philippians 1:6-7

     I can't tell you the exact moment the thought entered my mind or where it came from. What I do know is that in 2012, I found myself attempting suicide twice that year. I was a classic case. No one suspected a thing. I literally would go to work and church smiling. I was even making jokes. Then, I was literally going home thinking of ways to kill myself. After the second time, I stood up in church to testify. I didn't know what was going to come out of my mouth. However, I heard myself say, "The enemy told me to kill myself, and I tried." I surprised myself because I never had any intention of revealing my ugly truth. My mom was sitting in the audience. It was her first time hearing it, and I never intended for her to find out. I thank God for delivering me. I know two things today. One, the enemy knew what God had planned for me to do, and it would impact the kingdom. Two, God would use this experience that was meant for evil to work out for my good. If you're experiencing suicidal thoughts, seek God and seek help. Don't suffer in silence. Life is worth living, even in our darkest hours. There is a plan; trust the process.

Use the space below to write about how this devotional made you feel. Have you survived a situation like this? What changes do you think you should make in your life?

_____

_____

_____

_____

_____
_____
_____
_____
_____
_____
_____
_____
_____
_____
_____
_____
_____
_____
_____
_____
_____
_____
_____
_____
_____
_____
_____
_____
_____
_____
_____
_____
_____
_____

Day 7
Proverbs 24:16

Britney Spears had a popular song in the 90s entitled, "Oops!... I Did It Again." In the song, she talks about falling for the same guy again. However, when I think about the title, I think about habits, sins, relationships, and mistakes that I vowed never to repeat but eventually did. This also reminds me of Apostle Paul. He wrote three scriptures that always stick out to me. In 1 Tim 1:15, he calls himself the Chief Sinner. In Romans 7:19, he admits that he wants to do good, but evil is always present. Lastly, in 2 Cor 12:9, he discusses when God tells him that His grace is sufficient. When pondering these scriptures, what I had to realize and what Paul may have realized is that we are saved by grace. Therefore, any sins I may commit can be forgiven. However, I also must be willing to repent and ask to be delivered. This is how I can avoid the "Oops!... I did it again" syndrome.

After we repent, ask for forgiveness, and seek deliverance, we must then learn to forgive ourselves. This is often a daunting task, and usually it is not easy. If we want to move forward, we must do as Paul said, "Forgetting those things that are behind, I press towards the mark." I can't move forward in my deliverance if I'm still rolling around in the unforgiveness of yesterday. God created you to be more than a conqueror. You absolutely can forgive yourself, even for what you feel is the unthinkable.

Use the space below to write about how this devotional made you feel. Have you survived a situation like this? What changes do you think you should make in your life?

_____

_____

_____

_____

_____

_____

_____

_____

_____

_____

_____

_____

_____

_____

_____

_____

_____

_____

_____

_____

_____

_____

_____

_____

_____

_____

Day 8

Hebrews 13:5

Hello, God!? Are you there? I feel like this particularly on days when NOTHING is going right. I even feel like this when life throws unexpected curveballs like death or ongoing trials that never seem to end. In these moments, I've felt like God has walked away from watching over me. When pondering these moments, I often picture a parent who is holding the hand of a toddler who is learning to walk. Eventually, the parent lets go to see if the child is going to walk or sit. I also see the toddler looking at the parent with a horrific look that says, "Please don't let go." How often have you viewed yourself as the toddler and God as the parent?

I speculate that this is where many millennials walk away from God. Instead of relying on and believing in what we have been biblically taught, we resort to the fight-or-flight system that the world adheres to ever so often. When we assume the world's answer, our situation becomes more entangled than ever, and more devastation is surely on the horizon. The scripture in today's devotional assures us that God will never leave or forsake us. We must realize that in the moment when we feel like we're the toddler and God is the parent, He is letting go and watching to see if we will push forth in faith or sit down and retreat in fear. Trust God and the process instead of the way your circumstances appear.

Use the space below to write about how this devotional made you feel. Have you survived a situation like this? What changes do you think you should make in your life?

_____
_____
_____
_____
_____
_____
_____
_____
_____
_____
_____
_____
_____
_____
_____
_____
_____
_____
_____
_____
_____
_____
_____
_____
_____
_____
_____
_____
_____
_____

Day 9
Revelations 21:4

I recently lost my grandfather to complications from Alzheimer's. Like most elders, he was a source of strength for our family. Most of our family members attribute our work ethics and sense of family to him. Although we knew his death was inevitable, it was still a hard pill to swallow. No matter if the death was expected, tragic, or horrific, it's a tough situation and never easy to talk about. Not only can it cause grief, but it can also cause division among family members. It can make us rehash old memories and family secrets. Financial woes may be inherited or created by death. All these scenarios are quite hurtful. However, the most damaging thing I have seen death do is to cause people to lose their faith. When faith is lost, hope is also lost.

Sadly, many people have walked away from God because they just didn't understand why their loved one had to die. Maybe they assumed that walking away from God would lessen the pain. On the contrary, it would only cause more. God can heal any hurt that we may experience, if only we would believe and trust in Him. He can restore your hope and revive your faith. Keep holding on to God's unchanging hand. Death does not get the final say in your faith.

Use the space below to write about how this devotional made you feel. Have you survived a situation like this? What changes do you think you should make in your life?

_____
_____
_____
_____
_____
_____
_____
_____
_____
_____
_____
_____
_____
_____
_____
_____
_____
_____
_____
_____
_____
_____
_____
_____
_____
_____
_____
_____
_____
_____

Day 10
Isaiah 43:19

A couple of months ago, I was having a conversation with a coworker about church. We were discussing why people were leaving. We talked about the "philosophy" of the Bible. One of the points we were discussing was that the letter "J" was not yet a part of the alphabet when Jesus was born. As the discussion progressed, I began to compare and contrast religion - especially Christianity - from a Millennial's point of view versus that of a Baby Boomer. The one element that stood out above all else was the lack of questioning our grandparents did when it came to the Bible and Christianity.

I believe that the biggest mistakes the older saints or Baby Boomers made in church was to not ask questions and to rely heavily on what the pastor said. They took the pastor's word at face value. In certain churches, we weren't taught about the lost books of the bible nor was the Holy Trinity properly explained. For years, I thought the Holy Spirit was something that you "caught" and if not, He caused you to shout. It wasn't until I was an adult (and in a different sector of Christianity) that I learned that the Holy Spirit is not caught but received, and that the evidence is speaking in tongues not shouting. Most importantly, I was taught that the true reason for receiving the Holy Spirit is to learn holiness.

How did I learn these things? I learned them through regular attendance of bible study and asking questions. Millennials are not really hung upon traditions; unfortunately, that's what a lot of church rituals and services are based upon. Are you identifying yourself in a church of this system? This may be the reason you're bored with church and God. Remember that you are responsible for your own spiritual growth. If you're tired of tradition and you're not growing spiritually, then it's time to move on from that church. If you can repeat your pastor's sermon word for word, if you're the youngest thing in the church, if you're seeing more babies being born than weddings in church, it's time to move. This decision may be painful because you attend a family church, but don't allow tradition to hinder your growth. Choose wisely and ask God to lead you to the ministry that will fulfill your needs. Just like someone takes control of their health by diet changes, we must take control of our spiritual health as well. The spiritual, emotional, and physical health are one.

Use the space below to write about how this devotional made you feel. Have you survived a situation like this? What changes do you think you should make in your life?

_____

_____

_____

_____

_____

_____

_____

_____

_____

_____

_____

_____

_____

_____
_____
_____
_____
_____
_____
_____
_____
_____
_____
_____
_____
_____
_____
_____
_____
_____
_____
_____
_____
_____
_____
_____
_____
_____
_____
_____

Day 11
Proverbs 18:24

Admittedly, I'm not exactly the friendliest person. My personality traits can sometimes be described as mean or moody. These traits are an oxymoron when it comes to me being a Christian. I could get defensive and argue that my behaviors have been triggered by betrayal and abandonment in friendships. However, who hasn't experienced these actions in relationships as well as friendships? My truth is that because I'm not friendly and approachable, I often find myself alone. This is not a recipe for a fulfilling life. The bottom line is that we all need someone in our lives. We should all have at least one good friend. Jesus shouldn't be your only friend.

Why do we need friends? Well, they can hold us accountable for our actions. They can be a voice of reason. Sometimes friends are a source of entertainment as well as inspiration. They are needed to give us a different outlook and perspective of life. Prayer partners are often found in our friends. That's why we must be attentive to who we allow into our space (that's another devotional for another day). Don't allow past experiences to taint the new and wonderful experiences that lie ahead. God never intended for us to be alone. He even tells us to forsake not the gathering of ourselves together. He knew that we would definitely need the support of one another. Even God enjoyed the company of man. Why do you think you were created? Selah (Think about it.)

Use the space below to write about how this devotional made you feel. Have you survived a situation like this? What changes do you think you should make in your life?

_____

_____

_____

_____

_____

_____

_____

_____

_____

_____

_____

_____

_____

_____

_____

_____

_____

_____

_____

_____

_____

_____

_____

_____

_____

Day 12
Amos 3:3
Psalms 55

When I first entered the field of histology years ago, I had to be trained. The older histology technicians would tell the trainees, "It's not the quantity of slides you cut; it's the quality." In other words, I could cut a million slides, but if none of them could help the doctor come up with a diagnosis, then I essentially wasted my patient's tissue, my efforts, and the doctor's time producing that slide. However, if I took my time and gave a quality slide, then everyone involved in the patient's care could and would be happy. This same philosophy can be applied to friendship.

Thinking about friendship took me back to my middle school days. I was a nerd; I wasn't really popular with the students but more so popular with the teachers. At the beginning of every school year, there was a huge group of girls who hung together. Just like clockwork, every year they would argue and then physically fight. I always wondered did they not remember what happened last year. Why would they continue to hangout with those people for all that to happen again? It still boggles me until this day. I learned early on that having a lot of friends doesn't make you feel loved. In fact, some of the loneliest people in the world are surrounded by a crowd of friends.

Keep in mind that everyone who says they're your friend is not. At this time in a millennial's life, we should have learned the difference between coworker, associate, and friend. True friendships are usually recognized during times of crises and circumstances that will in no shape or form benefit your friend. If that person can withstand dire circumstances and remain your friend, you should keep that person around. Evaluate your friends list and ask yourself if they are adding to you or depleting you. Is the friendship one-sided? Are you always there for them but they're never there for you? Are you always in their cheering section, yet your bleachers are empty of them? Are you their bank, but when you need something, they are null and void? Remember that the amount of time you have been friends should not play a part in their role as a true friend. Judas walked with Jesus for three years. Do you recall how that worked out?

Use the space below to write about how this devotional made you feel. Have you survived a situation like this? What changes do you think you should make in your life?

_____

_____

_____

_____

_____

_____

_____

_____

_____

_____

_____

_____

_____

_____

_____

_____

Day 13

Romans 5:3-5

We all have had some form of struggle in our lives. We may have struggled with our finances, health, an addiction, and maybe even relationships. Regardless, the one thing that all struggles have is a lesson and an expiration date. The *when* and the *how* of learning the lesson so that the expiration date can come is totally left up to us. Character development also happens during this time. Patience, money management, faith, and longsuffering are all characteristics that can be obtained during this time. Nothing we go through is by accident or happenstance. We must learn to be grateful for our struggles. I understand that that is a hard concept to grasp. *Be grateful in our struggle?* Well, what other way can God cultivate you into the person that He needs you to be? How can you be ready for the dream and vision that you have for your life?

You learn to be more appreciative of things when you've had to struggle to earn them. The faster we catch on to embracing the struggle, the more character is built. Furthermore, the expiration date won't be prolonged, and the lesson won't have to be repeated. Think about the struggles you may have faced or the ones that you are currently facing. Have you had this same struggle before? Are you still in the same struggle? How long have you been there? Are you learning anything? Have you changed any of your ways? How has your attitude been during the struggle? After asking yourself these questions, reread the first paragraph, and get a clear definition of where you are going wrong. Then, ask God to help you adjust your mindset. Finally, get back in the race knowing that the only way is up from here. You were made to conquer not sit in defeat!

Use the space below to write about how this devotional made you feel. Have you survived a situation like this? What changes do you think you should make in your life?

_____

_____

_____

_____

_____

_____

_____

_____

_____

_____

_____

_____

_____

_____

_____

_____

_____

_____

_____

_____

_____

_____

_____

Day 14
1 Corinthians 13:4-5

This is going to be a touchy subject, and that's okay. Whether it was in a romantic relationship, friendship, or parental relationship, we all have experienced hurt. If you're anything like me, you tend to forgive and forget just to set yourself up to be hurt again. Now, I'm not telling you not to forgive, nor am I saying feed them with a long-handled spoon. However, what I am saying is that forgiveness DOES NOT equal relationship. In other words, I can forgive your actions, but I do not have be in your presence any longer. God himself had to tell me this once about a former friend. He said, "You're just not going to learn your lesson with them, are you?"

The bible does tell us to turn the other cheek, but it doesn't say to be a doormat or fool for anyone. God's love does not hurt. So, why should we accept hurtful so-called love from other people? Hurt could be physical, emotional, verbal, or psychological. I don't care what form it is given; it is all wrong. Take inventory of your life and relationships. If you feel like you're being hurt or put down, then you have a choice to make - stay and deal or leave and heal. It's your decision.

Use the space below to write about how this devotional made you feel. Have you survived a situation like this? What changes do you think you should make in your life?

_____
_____
_____

Day 15
Proverbs 1:15

I've always marched to the beat of a different drummer. My drummer might be slightly off beat, and likely wearing a different uniform from the rest of the band. I never intended to be like this, but I know God has a sense of humor. I never really fit in at school or church. What I had to learn is that I'm not a loner. Instead, I'm a leader. Even as adults, we still try to fit in. Only now, it's called keeping up with the Joneses. I once had a classmate tell me, "Girl, we thought you moved out of town. We never see you out." She was correct.

I've never done what is considered normal for my peers to do. I don't go to clubs. I don't have children. I stopped drinking, and I really don't hang out with people my age. Instead, I'm active in church. I'm focused on my career, and I hang with women twice my age. My sister often tells me I'm an old woman. I like to think I have an old soul. Perhaps you're feeling left out and left behind by your peers. Maybe their interests aren't your interests, and that's okay, too. Sometimes, if not all the time, it's best to take the road less traveled.

Use the space below to write about how this devotional made you feel. Have you survived a situation like this? What changes do you think you should make in your life?

_____

_____

_____

_____

_____
_____
_____
_____
_____
_____
_____
_____
_____
_____
_____
_____
_____
_____
_____
_____
_____
_____
_____
_____
_____
_____
_____
_____
_____
_____
_____
_____
_____

Day 16

Habakkuk 2:2

When I was growing up in church, the only time I heard about dreams usually pertained to stories about God speaking to His servants. It wasn't until I was older (I mean really grown) that I heard and read a scripture that spoke volumes to my situation. Dream-chasing and goal-aspiring couldn't be put any clearer in the scripture that accompanies this devotional. Mediocrity to you should be like kryptonite is to Superman: poison that leads to death. Everyone should have some a goal or aspiration. Without either, you will perish or be simply existing instead of living.

No dream is too big or too small. Stop putting limits on yourself and, most importantly, God. The one thing that we should be sure of is that our dreams are aligned with God's plan for our lives. Too often, we follow visions and dreams that were never given to us by God. Your vision or dream should not be powered by greed. Those dreams rarely come to fruition. Instead, be driven by passion and belief in your dream. Wake up, wipe the sleep from your eyes, and begin to chase your dreams. It's never too late to get started!

Use the space below to write about how this devotional made you feel. Have you survived a situation like this? What changes do you think you should make in your life?

_____

_____

_____

_____
_____
_____
_____
_____
_____
_____
_____
_____
_____
_____
_____
_____
_____
_____
_____
_____
_____
_____
_____
_____
_____
_____
_____
_____
_____
_____
_____
_____

Reflection

We're a little past the halfway point in the devotional, which means we're well into our 30-day journey. I hope I've said something thus far that will at least make you pause or think before leaving church or God. If not, I urge you to continue reading. Remember that God has appointed times for all things.

Day 17

John 10:10

In the last devotional, I mentioned living or existing. When I think of living, I think of vibrance, embracing new adventures, chasing dreams and visions, and being joyful and happy. Existing is the exact opposite. It's joylessness - not being excited about life or facing new days. Instead, it's about just waiting to get through the day. Many Christians find themselves existing and not living. God never intended this for His children.

Take inventory of your life. Think about how you went through yesterday or today. Did you smile? Did you have a song in your heart? Did you work on your dream? Have you had a genuine laugh today? If you answered no, then think back and recall when you lost your joy. When did you began existing instead of living? What circumstance or situation brought you to this place? Perhaps this may be one of the reasons you've lost your joy and hope in God. When you get to the root of this matter, it may solve all the other issues at hand. Pray and ask God to identify the root of your problem, and then ask Him to restore what you've lost. You can't find happiness or joy in another person. It must come from within. Most importantly, it must start with your relationship with God.

Use the space below to write about how this devotional made you feel. Have you survived a situation like this? What changes do you think you should make in your life?

_____

_____

_____
_____
_____
_____
_____
_____
_____
_____
_____
_____
_____
_____
_____
_____
_____
_____
_____
_____
_____
_____
_____
_____
_____
_____
_____
_____
_____
_____
_____

Day 18
Ephesians 6:11-18

Many years ago, I worked for a clinical and anatomical pathology laboratory on the night crew. A time came when we were not getting along (it was bad). The company decided to call in an expert to get to the root of our issues. Our skills coach broke down our shift and discovered that we had three different generations working together: Baby Boomers, Generation X, and Millennials. In each, group she highlighted unique qualities about that generation. However, when she got to the millennials, I was absolutely floored by the discovery. According to the expert, millennials have never known peace because the country has been at war since we graced planet Earth. After hearing this, I began to reflect.

How many people have felt like this since giving their life to Christ? I've personally heard several people say that they had more peace when they were in the world than when they became saved. This is an illusion sent from the enemy himself. The reason you felt at peace is because you were on the enemy's side. He didn't have a reason to bother you. If you were so much at peace, then what made you feel like you were missing something that made you give your life to Christ? The minute you gave your life to Christ, the enemy immediately had a vendetta against you. His job is to kill, steal, and destroy you in any way possible. He knows the benefits of you serving God; he once had those same benefits. Therefore, if you're feeling like you're in a constant battle, it's because you are.

We have to fight to keep ourselves on the winning team. Think about it in the physical realm. If someone were continuously attacking you, wouldn't you fight back? No one would stand and allow someone to pummel them. The enemy fights you in all realms: physical, spiritual, and emotional, and he doesn't fight fairly. That's why we need the Trinity. We need God the Father in front, God the Son in the back, and God the Holy Spirit covering all sides.

Use the space below to write about how this devotional made you feel. Have you survived a situation like this? What changes do you think you should make in your life?

_____

_____

_____

_____

_____

_____

_____

_____

_____

_____

_____

_____

_____

_____

_____

_____

_____

_____

_____

Day 19

Matthew 18:15

I already know I'm going to ruffle some feathers with this one. You may even choose to dislike me after this, but here we go. One day I was scrolling on Facebook and I saw a post of a young lady at the welfare office. She was carrying a designer bag and her son had on expensive tennis shoes. The caption of the post said: "Setting our priorities straight." I liked the post and then reposted. Here's where the issue inserts itself… Later that day, I got back on Facebook and saw that someone I loved and trusted had ripped me to shreds because of that post. I mean, they put all my business about my marriage and everything on Facebook. I was hurt because my post was not about them, but they took it personally.

Instead of being an adult and addressing the person and the issue, I cut myself off from them (social media and all) and never spoke to them again. This wasn't an easy task because we ran in the same circle. Our relationship was beyond repair, yet as a Christian, I could still pray for them as well as be there for them. I said all that to say this: 1. If a relationship can be repaired, don't allow pride to get in the way. 2. Be careful of your words; they can be forgiven but not so easily forgotten. I don't regret making the post; however, I do regret not addressing the issue with the individual and making peace. Life is too short. Love hard and forgive quickly.

Use the space below to write about how this devotional made you feel. Have you survived a situation like this? What changes do you think you should make in your life?

_____
_____
_____
_____
_____
_____
_____
_____
_____
_____
_____
_____
_____
_____
_____
_____
_____
_____
_____
_____
_____
_____
_____
_____
_____
_____
_____
_____
_____
_____

Day 20
Job 14

I am learning that life is full of issues. We cause some issues ourselves, and life simply gives us others. No matter how the issue comes about, one thing is abundantly clear: we choose how we go through our problems. The first thing we must realize in dealing with our problems is that they're inevitable. There's no getting away from that; it's life. The second thing we must come to terms with is finding a way to endure the problem. Let's zero in on the second part.

In my experiences, I have chosen to ignore the problem. I would sleep all the time or immerse myself in life simulation games (ironic I know) in order to avoid thinking about the situation. I would completely avoid talking to anyone because the conversation would likely force me to talk about my problem. What I am learning now is that avoidance is never the answer. Avoidance is just another avenue or pathway for fear to set up. Unhealthy fear in the Christian life is unacceptable. To combat avoidance and fear, I learned to pray and praise. I know it sounds cliché, but I promise it helps so much.

What I had to learn with avoidance is that it only compounded the problem. It not only led to fear, but then I began to have anxiety. I had to learn that I could talk about the problem to the only person who could help me solve it…God. It didn't matter to Him if I had caused this issue myself or if it was just life handing me lemons. His only concerned was that I learned to bring EVERYTHING to Him FIRST. When I prayed about the situation and brought it to Him, I didn't have to be fearful of it being repeated (which was part of the fear and anxiety). Moreover, I knew there was an answer waiting for me.

If you're having a problem, you can either be weary and worry or pray and praise. I also learned that when I pray and praise, it takes my mind and energy off the problem. Some would say this is another avoidance tactic. However, avoidance doesn't produce results, but prayer and praise always do. Peace during your problems is a byproduct of prayer and praise. Determine now how you're going to finish going through this problem. Lay it at the feet of Jesus and leave it there. Mind over matter. Prayer and praise.

Use the space below to write about how this devotional made you feel. Have you survived a situation like this? What changes do you think you should make in your life?

_____

_____

_____

_____

_____

_____

_____

_____

_____

_____

_____

_____

_____

_____

Day 21
Romans 3:23

One of the biggest mistakes we make in life is placing people on pedestals and then expecting them to live up to unrealistic expectations. This is one of the many ways we set ourselves up for disappointments. In my opinion, this is why many people are leaving the church. We have placed Godlike faith in man instead of who it really should be in which is God. Too often, our faith is shattered or shaken when our church leaders are found in less than favorable circumstances. However, they're not God.

Consider this analogy: The church is the hospital for physical, emotional, and mental illnesses. We're all in the hospital because we need to heal on some level. Well people are not in the hospital. Here's where we get into trouble… We get the hierarchy of the "medical team" out of order. We, the members of the church, are the patients. Our pastors and leaders are the nurses, not the doctors! The Holy Trinity is our doctor. Why? Because the Holy Trinity is the head of the church, not your pastor. Think about it. When you're being treated at the hospital, it is not the nurse who prescribes your course of treatment. The doctor does that. This is also true for the church. It is God who tells your leaders what you need to hear concerning the word of God. It is God who tells your pastor what the saints of God are going through. Even the nurse has to see the doctor from time to time.

If your faith has been so shaken up by what's going on with your leaders and pastors, then you may need to question yourself on who your faith is really in. It should be in God always. Even God tells us we will fall short of His glory because we're human. Yes, God made us in His image, but we have to ask for the mind of Christ. Stop letting everything in church mess with your sensibility. No one is perfect, and that includes your leaders. Forgive them just as God forgives you, and then place your faith in the only one who will not fail or disappoint you. Jesus!

Use the space below to write about how this devotional made you feel. Have you survived a situation like this? What changes do you think you should make in your life?

_____

_____

_____

_____

_____

_____

_____

_____

_____

_____

_____

_____

_____

_____

_____

_____

_____

_____

_____

Day 22

Ecclesiastes 3:1-8

You're so close to the end of this devotional, but you still have a decision to make about your spiritual life. *Should I walk away from church and God? Should I just walk away from church? Maybe I should just stay and press my way through to the end of this path of life.* God has given each and every one of us free will. He will not force Christianity or himself upon us. In this freewill, He allows us to make the decision to love and follow Him. I want you to think past the hardships you're facing right now. Redirect your focus on all the good times you've had in your relationship with God. Think about all the impossible situations that you faced and didn't know how you were going to make it out. Guess what. This time is no different. The test maybe a little harder, but at the end of the day, it's still just that - a test. If God didn't leave you when you dealt with all the other circumstances, why would He leave you now?

The issue with millennials is that we're a microwave generation. We want things fast, quick, and in a hurry. I'm very guilty of this trait myself. I wanted the Lord to allow me to write a 30-day devotional in a week - *a week.* How crazy is that? Then, I wanted to shorten it to a 10-day devotional because I didn't want to stay in the press for the other twenty days. Your desire for your situation to be fixed in a hurry is no different from my desire to finish a book in a week. What you and I must realize is that in this time, God wants to cultivate something within us or retrieve something from us. Whatever it is, we must trust God and His timing.

Use the space below to write about how this devotional made you feel. Have you survived a situation like this? What changes do you think you should make in your life?

_____
_____
_____
_____
_____
_____
_____
_____
_____
_____
_____
_____
_____
_____
_____
_____
_____
_____
_____
_____
_____
_____
_____
_____
_____
_____
_____
_____
_____

Day 23
Ephesians 5:22-23

You know what I'm sick of seeing? The hashtag relationship goals (#relationship goals). We are wanting to base our relationships on other people's surface glimpses that they allow others to see in their relationships. They show pictures of themselves on lavish vacations or pictures of them engaging in fancy meals wearing fancy clothes. We don't have a clue of what really goes on behind closed doors, but we want to be like them. This bothers me to no end. Why? Who's to say if that couple is truly happy? How much debt are they in living that life? Who's to say that they're really even a couple? Hmm….

We can't base any of our relationships on others. Rather, our relationships should be based on our connection with God. A preacher once said, "If you want to know how someone is going to treat you, watch their relationship with God." I wish I would have known this advice years ago. It would have saved many days of heartache. It is okay to ask others for advice. Remember that every relationship is different. Still, chasing God should be everyone's relationship goals. One thing I strive to do daily is to model any relationship I engage in, whether it's friendships or relationships, with the relationship I have with God. In other words, I try to treat people the way that I treat God. I'm not saying I make the mark every time. Most often, I don't even get close to the mark, but that is my goal. It took me a while to figure this out, but like the saying goes, it's better late than never.

Use the space below to write about how this devotional made you feel. Have you survived a situation like this? What changes do you think you should make in your life?

_____
_____
_____
_____
_____
_____
_____
_____
_____
_____
_____
_____
_____
_____
_____
_____
_____
_____
_____
_____
_____
_____
_____
_____
_____
_____
_____
_____

Day 24

1 Corinthians 7:32-35

I get it. You really want to be married. I've been there. I was thirty-three when I got married, and I ignored the signs that we weren't ready. I don't want you to make that same mistake. The reality is that we liked the idea of marriage and not the work of marriage. Yes, marriage is work! Although I waited awhile to marry, I did not use my time as a single woman wisely. My truth is that I really didn't know who I was. I did not know or recognize my full potential. My personal belief is that I hadn't done all that I needed to do as a single Christian woman. Friends warned me time and time again that I wasn't ready for marriage, but I charged ahead anyway. As a result, I'm in a predicament that could have been avoided had I heeded the warnings.

I know that you're tired of being single. I understand that, but you don't want to rush into something that might not last. Instead of being frustrated about your singleness, embrace it. Reach your full potential as a single person in God. Find your ministry and work. God knows your desire, and He will give you your desires. However, remember to trust God's timing. Our timing leads to mistakes. I literally need you to take a page from my book and don't get ahead of God.

Use the space below to write about how this devotional made you feel. Have you survived a situation like this? What changes do you think you should make in your life?

———————————————————————————
———————————————————————————
———————————————————————————

_____
_____
_____
_____
_____
_____
_____
_____
_____
_____
_____
_____
_____
_____
_____
_____
_____
_____
_____
_____
_____
_____
_____
_____
_____
_____
_____
_____
_____
_____
_____

Day 25

Isaiah 55:8-9

A group of coworkers was talking and about their lives. They were discussing their past and present circumstances. The conversation ranged from marriage to finances. One coworker had absolutely NOTHING positive to say about her life. In her eyes, nothing seemed to be going right in her life. However, when the other coworker gave a possible solution, there was always an excuse as to why it wouldn't work. In frustration, the coworker who was giving advice walked off.

It's one thing to see the issues in your life, but you have to be open to resolving your problems. The truth of the matter is a lot of us use our problems as crutches. As long as God allows breath in your body, you have the potential to make your life better. When God is giving you solutions, and you choose not to apply them, you're simply telling Him you give up! This is called the "defeated life syndrome." There are too many Christians living defeated joyless lives. That is an oxymoron when it comes to Christianity. If you're unhappy or life is not what it could be for you, then do some soul searching. Ask God to reveal your purpose. It's never too late to change your career. It's never too late to pursue your dreams. We have to make the decision to take off the garment of mourning and put on the garment of praise. If we don't change our mindsets, we will find ourselves on the sidelines of life watching everyone else playing the game of life.

Use the space below to write about how this devotional made you feel. Have you survived a situation like this? What changes do you think you should make in your life?

_____

_____

_____

_____

_____

_____

_____

_____

_____

_____

_____

_____

_____

_____

_____

_____

_____

_____

_____

_____

_____

_____

_____

_____

_____

_____

_____

_____

_____

_____

Day 26

2 Timothy 1:7

Fear has two acronyms: **F**ace **E**verything **A**nd **R**ise or **F**orget **E**verything **A**nd **R**un. More than I care to admit, I've often operated in the latter instead of the first. Lack of faith in God as well as myself led me to making disastrous decisions. The Bible plainly tells us that God did not give us fear in the negative. So where does fear come from? It comes from the enemy. What's the objective of fear? Fear is used to keep the people of God bound. It keeps us from operating in our full potential in God. We miss opportunities because of fear. We won't step out in faith because of fear. It can also cause spiritual, emotional, and physical death in the Christian life.

I can personally attest to how fear kept me from traveling, doing ministry, and fulfilling my purpose. Ask God to reveal those areas in your life that are masking themselves as safe decisions rather than being what they really are, which is fear. After they are revealed, pray that fear is replaced with faith. You have too much to do to allow it to keep you bound. Remember that you're more than a conqueror through Jesus Christ.

Use the space below to write about how this devotional made you feel. Have you survived a situation like this? What changes do you think you should make in your life?

_____
_____
_____
_____

Day 27
Genesis 3:8-10

We live in a day and time where people are not authentically themselves. We are in the age of virtual reality where we can create an alter ego. We can live fictious lives portraying to be one thing to the world yet having a totally different life in reality. We hide behind social media, jobs, families, money, and all things physical. We even hide behind religion. Some of us are hiding behind our pain, our past, and our sufferings instead of dealing with our issues. The things we aren't hiding from, we're running from instead. Some of us are running from our realities, our responsibilities, our issues, and our callings. Some of us are even running from God.

Stop running and answer the call from God. It's only then that we can stop hiding from our issues. Furthermore, we can truly be ourselves authentically. Why? God loves us in spite of ourselves. He created us, and He knows us. God will cover us while we get ourselves together. He won't expose the image we have been portraying if we confess and repent. He's the only one who can clean us up from the inside out. Let go and allow Him to put you back on the potter's wheel and mold you into who He desires you to be.

Use the space below to write about how this devotional made you feel. Have you survived a situation like this? What changes do you think you should make in your life?

_____

_____

Day 28
1 Corinthians 12:14-24

This is the only devotional that involves several scriptures. I needed each of these scriptures to relay a very important message. The message is this: The body of Christ needs you. Think about your talent. Are you a good singer? Do you write poems? Are you personable? Do you like helping others? These talents play an active role in ministry. Now, when I say ministry, I don't necessarily mean the preaching ministry. However, our talents that God instilled in us are supposed to be used to minister to others. You may not feel that serving is a talent, but it is. In fact, it is one of the key elements in Christianity. Christ came here to serve, not to be served. If we would read the gospel, we would see Christ either feeding, praying, or caring for those in need. That's what were called to do.

I have found that when I'm going through a rough patch, it is always in my best interest to take the focus off myself and place it on others. Christians should not be selfish. Withholding your gift from the body of Christ is a selfish act, and it's a direct defiance. If we choose not to use what God has given us, He always has someone else who is willing and available to be used by Him. Your unwillingness to work will not stop the body of Christ from moving forward. However, it may stop your plans in the spiritual and physical realm. When we are outside the will of God, we are outside the blessing lane. Do parents reward bad behavior? Are treats given to disobedient children? We cannot tell God no and believe that the fruit of our hands will be blessed. A very powerful woman once said that when she leaves this Earth, she wants to be empty of all the gifts that God gave her because she used them all for His glory. That's an awesome way to look at life. Why not use all you have for the one person who gave it all to you?

Use the space below to write about how this devotional made you feel. Have you survived a situation like this? What changes do you think you should make in your life?

_____

_____

_____

_____

_____

_____

_____

_____

_____

_____

_____

_____

_____

_____

_____

_____

_____

_____

_____

_____

_____

_____

_____

_____

Day 29

2 Timothy 3:16
John 10:27-28

The point of this devotional is to get you to strengthen your relationship with God. One of the ways this can be done is through consistent bible study and prayer. This approach can help us get to know God on a deeper level. We can find direction for our lives in the word of God. We also get to know the promises of God as we hear and begin to know His voice. There was a time when I really didn't know the voice of the Lord for myself. I think that's a lot of our issues today. We won't get in the presence of the Lord long enough to hear Him. Praying has become a monologue instead of a dialogue. Understand that prayer is not a wish list, and God is not Santa. Instead, prayer is a two-way conversation or dialogue between yourself and God. He desires to spend time with us just as a father desires to spend time with His child.

Another reason we need to learn to hear the voice of the Lord is because there are false prophets lurking. When we are immature in the things of God, which comes from lack of communication with Him, we are vulnerable to the lying, deceiving tongue of the enemy. False prophets prey on those who know very little or nothing at all about the word of God. When you read your bible and know the voice of the Lord, discernment becomes a part of your makeup, and you begin to recognize when someone is "prophe-lying" to you. Reading this devotional has placed you at a good start with consistent bible studying and praying. If you've never heard the voice of the Lord before,

I'm sure you've heard it now. Stay on this path and watch the growth that will come forth in your life.

Use the space below to write about how this devotional made you feel. Have you survived a situation like this? What changes do you think you should make in your life?

_____

_____

_____

_____

_____

_____

_____

_____

_____

_____

_____

_____

_____

_____

_____

_____

_____

_____

_____

_____

_____

_____

_____

_____

_____

_____

Day 30

2 Timothy 4:7-8

You should be so proud of yourself. You've made it to the last devotional. Even though this signifies the end, it's just the beginning of your new start. I'm sure this road was not easy. Trust me; it wasn't easy writing it. But, by the Grace of God, you and I have survived. We've finished our course! During this 30-day journey, I hope you've discovered new things about your relationship with God and about yourself. I pray that you fell in love all over again with who you are as a person. I pray that you tapped into the true potential that's within you as a believer of Christ. Hopefully, I have conveyed to you that you're not the only who's struggle with this decision that's before you. God heard the cry of your heart, and He entrusted me to write the answer He gave. I want you to celebrate this moment! You deserve it! I'm sure that while reading this devotional, you had to drudge up some embarrassments, bad decisions, and more than likely some pain. Nevertheless, you came out on the other side as a winner! It doesn't matter if you stopped and then started again. You finished strong! To God be the Glory for the things that He has done!

So, what's next…

You have to decide. Do you stay, or do you leave? Which direction will you go from here? If you're still not sure, I suggest you reread the devotional for another thirty days and go over your notes. If you feel led, go on a fast and ask God to speak to your heart and mind. I know the true answer is to stay with God because I was once at this crossroad myself. However, I can't tell you what to do, just as God won't force himself or His will onto you. Just the same, I won't force my beliefs and opinion onto you. The choice has always been and will always be yours. Be blessed.

Use the space below to write about how this devotional made you feel. Have you survived a situation like this? What changes do you think you should make in your life?

_____

_____

_____

_____

_____

_____

_____

_____

_____

_____

_____

_____

_____

_____

_____

_____

_____

_____

_____

_____

_____

www.ingramcontent.com/pod-product-compliance
Lightning Source LLC
LaVergne TN
LVHW011338080426
835513LV00006B/426